MARITAL RAPE

VOLUME 2, ISSUE 1 OF BRILLOPEDIA

KUMARI MUSKAN

ISBN 979-888606941-9

Contents

Preface

"Start writing, no matter what. The water does not flow until the faucet is turned on".

-Louis L'Amour

Hundreds of students and professors are contributing their work to Brillopedia, we are here to provide ample information about Law and Contemporary issues. Our aim is to provide a platform for today's generation to express their views and ideas on law and contemporary law.

Publication

This research paper is published in volume 2, issue 1 of Brillopedia

Author

Kumari Muskan

CHAPTER ONE

ABSTRACT

Sexual violence is defined as the act of exposing a person to sexual behavior without the consent of the individual. It involves many behaviors ranging from touching to rape. Most victims are women. Rape is an act having sex with a person without his or her consent. The concept of marital rape has been largely ignored years because of ideas that encourage men who have the right to treat their wives the way they wish and the wife should provide for her husband with all his needs. Today with the changes and advances in wedding ideas, I increased public awareness and understanding of the concept of violence against women; it is now he understood that sexual relations should be enjoyed by both parties. Otherwise should be regarded as sexual harassment / violence.

The purpose of this article is to review the medical, social, and legal aspects of marital rape, presenting what is happening now situation regarding marital rape in Turkey and around the world, to discuss how to prevent it.

CHAPTER TWO

INTRODUCTION

Marital rape or rape of a spouse is a sexual act with a spouse without the consent of his or her partner. Lack of a permit is an important factor and there is no need to engage in physical violence. Marital rape is considered a form of domestic violence and sexual assault. Although, historically, sexuality was viewed as a marital right, sexual activity without the consent of one's mate is now widely categorized as rape in many societies around the world, international conventions are rejected, and crime is increasingly criminalized.

Stories of sexual violence and domestic violence in marriage and, in particular, the issue of violence against women, have reached increasing international attention since the second half of the 20th century. However, in many lands, marital rape is still illegal, or illegal, but widely tolerated. Laws are rarely enforced, due to factors ranging from the authorities' reluctance to pursue crime, and the lack of public awareness that sex outside of marriage is illegal.

Marital rape is more common among women, though not. Marital rape is often a form of unrelenting violence against the abuser that occurs in abusive relationships. It is available on a complex web of provincial governments, cultural practices, and community ideas that come together to influence every situation and situation in different ways. The skepticism about interpreting illicit sex between spouses as a crime and persecution has been fueled by popular perceptions about marriage, the interpretation of religious teachings, views on homosexuality, and the traditional expectations of a wife's subjection to her husband. -deeds that are still common in many parts of the world. These views on marriage and sexuality began to be challenged in many Western lands from the 1960s and 70s mainly on the feminist system, leading to the recognition of a woman's right to self-determination (that is, to control) all matters concerning her body.

and the withdrawal of the release or protection of marital rape.

Many countries criminalize marital rape from the late 20th century onward — very few legal systems allowed for the prosecution of marital rape prior to the 1970's. Crime crimes occur in a variety of ways, including the removal of legal exemptions from the definition of rape, sentencing decisions, a clear legal reference to a law prohibiting the use of marriage as a protection, or the creation of a specific rape case in marriage. In many lands, it is not yet clear that marital rape is linked to normal rape laws, but in some lands there is a criminal code that can be enforced under normal law to prevent violence, such as abuse and assault.

CHAPTER THREE

HISTORY

Historically, in most parts of the world, rape was considered a crime or theft of personal property (usually either husband or father). In this case, the destruction of property meant that the crime could not be legally recognized as damage to the victim, but rather the property of his father or her husband. Therefore, by definition a man could not rape his wife. The idea that a husband could not be blamed for raping his wife was explained by Sir Matthew Hale (1609-1676) in The History of the Pleas of the Crown, published after his death in 1736, in which he wrote that "the husband could not be guilty of rape. because, according to the agreement of the wife, she is bound to her husband, and he cannot divorce her." Also, American and English law applied until the 20th century in the secrecy system, that is, legal doctrine, in which, when married, a woman's legal rights were exercised by those of her husband. her marital status, rather than being charged with rape.

Multiple authorities, including all U.S. states fifty, had committed marital rape in the 1990s. Common English law has also had a profound effect on many of the world's legal systems through colonialism.

Kersti Yllö in the foreword to Understanding Marital Rape In a Global Context states, "In some cultures, consent is not even something that every woman can give. Families planning a marriage guarantee her permanent consent." Control over a particular man. a woman's sexuality was part of a larger control that men had in all other aspects of her life. Man's dominion over his wife's body is seen in the way adultery between a woman and another man; for example, in 1707, the English King Judge John Holt described the act of having sex with another man's wife as "the most serious assault on property". For this reason, in many cultures there was a conflict between cases of rape and adultery, as both were considered and understood as violations of the husband's rights. Spouse rape was considered a property crime against the husband, not against the woman's right to self-determination.

The property to be reserved for a woman was her virginity; this was an asset (Bergen, 2016). Following this line of reasoning, the woman was (and still is in many cultures around the world) first the property of her father, and then, in marriage, her husband's property (Bergen, 2016). Therefore, a man could not be prosecuted for raping his wife because she was his property (Schelong, 1994). However, if another man raped a man's wife, this was actually a theft of property (female sex) (Bergen, 2016). According to English tradition, a "bride capture" (a man who claims to be a woman by rape) was thought to be stealing his father's property by raping his daughter. Therefore, rape laws were created "to protect the property rights that men had for their women, not to protect women themselves" (Schelong, 1994). This concept of women as property is full of current ideas and laws on marital rape around the world.

In some cultures, marriage is arranged with the intention of creating fertility (Yllö, 2016). In these cases, the parties do not actually agree to marry (in the case of a forced marriage) (Yllö, 2016). Following this concept, if consent is not part of the marriage, then it is not necessary to have sex. The independence of the wife is also often loosened in rituals where lobola is paid. Under customary law in some parts of Africa, forced sex in marriage was not forbidden, although certain specific circumstances, such as when pregnant, immediately after childbirth, during menstruation, or during mourning for a dead loved one, were considered offensive. the right to refuse sex.

Rape, until recently, was perceived as a crime against dignity and dignity - not only in domestic law, but also in international law; For example, according to Article 27 of the Fourth Geneva Convention, "Women shall be particularly protected by attacks from their own dignity, especially from rape, forced prostitution, and any other form of indecent assault." It was not until the 1990s that ICC law recognized the crime of sexual violence as a crime against humanity; [10] "It was not until the last half of the century that rape was perceived as a crime against a woman, her dignity, rather than against her family or her husband."

CHAPTER FOUR

LEGAL ASPECT

Historically, many cultures have envisioned the rights of married couples to have sex with each other. This can be seen in the common law in English, which applies to North America and the British Commonwealth, where the very idea of marital rape was considered impossible. This was made clear by Sir Matthew Hale, (1609-1676), in his official book Historia Placitorum Coronæ or History of the Pleas of the Crown (after his death, 1736) in which he wrote that "The Husband could not be guilty of rape. to his legal wife, because by mutual consent and agreement the wife has been so devoted to her husband, she will not be able to withdraw. "

<u>Legalizing an exemption from marital rape in law</u>

General law and United Kingdom

History of the Pleas of the Crown did not provide an official example of this, although it is based on earlier standards. In the case of Lord Audley (1488–1544), for example, Hale quotes a lawyer named Branton (c. 1210 - c. 1268) who supports this law, which is said to have been taken from the laws of King Æthelstan (r. 927–939) when the law insisted that even non-natives a healthy party, but they were prostitutes, yet there may be abuse: but it is good to say that she was his concubine". Legal marriage confirms the act of marriage itself, so "marital rape" is a conditional dispute. While physical abuse of a spouse may be charged, that is different from authorizing a marriage union such as rape. Then marriage should not be defined as "liberation" from rape but as "opposition" to it. Marriage creates marital rights between spouses, and marriage cannot be dissolved without an Act of Parliament — so it follows that the spouse could not revoke the marital rights, so there can be no rape between the spouses. The principle was repeated in the East's Treatise of the Pleas of the Crown in 1803 and in the Archbold's Pleading and Evidence in Criminal Cases in 1822. The law was enacted as an exemption from rape law in England court in the case of R v Clarence, but was not repealed until 1991 by the House of Lords in the case of R. v. R in 1991, where it was described as a legal myth that is inconsistent with offensive and offensive.

Criticism of women in the 19th century

From the beginning of the 19th century in the fight for women's rights, activists have challenged the so-called right of men to have sex with their wives. In the United States, "the nineteenth-century feminist movement fought for the right of the husband to control sexual relations in marriage in a campaign that was significantly improved, expanded, and persevered, given 19th-century obstacles to public discourse on gender or sexuality. Suffragists including Elizabeth Cady Stanton and Lucy Stone "chose a woman's right to control her marital status as a key component of equality."

Nineteenth-century demands for women focused on women's right to control their bodies and reproduction, permitted placement in marital sex as an alternative to contraception and abortion (which many opposed), and embraced eugenic concerns about overeating. British freedom fighters John Stuart Mill and Harriet Taylor have attacked marital rape as a double standard of law and the backbone of female subjugation. failure to confirm

Proponents of the Free Love Movement, which includes early anarcha-feminists such as Voltairine de Cleyre and Emma Goldman, as well as Victoria Woodhull, Thomas Low Nichols, and Mary Gove Nichols, have joined in condemning marital rape to represent women's independence and sexual pleasure. Moses Harman, a Kansas-based publisher and advocate for women's rights, has twice been arrested under Comstock laws for publishing articles (by a woman who was abused and a doctor who treated rape in marriage) condemning marital rape. De Cleyre defended Harman in a well-known article, "Sex Slavery." He refuses to make any distinction between rape outside and inside marriage: "And that is rape, when a man forcibly has sex with a woman whether he is legally authorized to do so or not."

Bertrand Russell (who was awarded the Nobel Prize for Literature in 1950) in his book Marriage and Morals (1929) spoke ill of married women. He wrote "Marriage is a woman's normal life-style, and the total amount of unwanted sex tolerated by women is probably greater in marriage than in fornication."

Crime of the 20th and 21st centuries

Release or protection from marital rape is widely regarded as inconsistent with the growing perception of human rights and equality.

Women have been working orderly since the 1960s to break free from marital rape and make marital rape a criminal offense. The escalation of the criminalization of the rape of a spouse is part of a global reorganization of sexual offenses "from cases of morality, family, morality, fame, or innocence ... to cases against freedom, self-determination, or physical integrity." December 1993, the United Nations High Commissioner for Human Rights published a Declaration on the Elimination of All Forms of Discrimination against Women. This proves marital rape as a violation of human rights.

The importance of the right to self-determination of women is increasingly recognized as a fundamental right to women's rights. In 2012, Chief Human Rights Commissioner Navi Pillay said so

"Violations of women's rights are often linked to gender and their reproductive role. (...) In many countries, married women may not refuse to have sexual relations with their husbands, and they often have no word on whether they use contraception. ...) Ensuring that women have full control over their bodies is an important first step in achieving a strong balance between women and men. who choose to have children — at the heart of a life of dignity."

Despite these international trends and measures, criminal activity has not yet taken place in all UN member states. Determining the criminal nature of marital rape can be challenging, because, although some countries make it a crime (by imposing on their rape laws that marriage is not a protection against rape cases; or by committing certain crimes of 'marital rape'; a spouse may be accused of raping his or her spouse) and other countries that may openly release their spouse (by defining rape as forced sexual intercourse outside of marriage; Many common rape laws do not address the issue (i.e., they do not address the issue in one way or another) —in those cases, to determine whether marital rape is minimal the common sense of rape should be considered if there are judicial decisions in this regard; and previous definitions of the law are also important (for example whether there was a legal release that was removed by the legislature for the purpose of explicitly incorporating marital rape).

In 2006, a comprehensive study by the UN Secretary-General on all forms of violence against women stated:

"Marital rape can be prosecuted in at least 104 countries. Of these, 32 have made marital rape a criminal offense, while the other 74 do not exempt marital rape from the norms of normal rape. Marital rape is not a prosecuted offense at least 53 it is the only case where the couple is legally separated. Four states are considering legislation that would allow marital rape to be prosecuted."

In 2011, a report by the UN Women's Progress of the World's Women: In Pursuit of Justice state:

"By April 2011, at least 52 states had openly banned marital rape in their criminal codes."

Traditionally, rape was a crime that could only be committed outside of marriage, and courts could not apply the principles of rape to forced sexual relations between spouses. With the change in social attitudes, as well as the worldwide condemnation of sexual violence in marriage, courts have begun to apply marital rape laws. The current application of marital rape laws is unclear at this time, as in many countries these laws have not been tested in court recently. In some countries, especially authorities who have inherited the Indian Penal Code (such as Singapore, India, Bangladesh, Sri Lanka, Burma) and in other countries in the Commonwealth Caribbean, laws openly release spouses from persecution (e.g., under the Constitution. 1860 Indian Penal Code, which has also been adopted by other countries in the region, rape law states "Sexual intercourse is not rape").

An example of a country where rape law explicitly excludes a husband as a possible perpetrator is Ethiopia; Its law of rape states: "Article 620 - Rape: Anyone who compels a woman to have sexual relations outside of marriage, by resorting to violence or intimidation, or after making her unconscious or unable to resist, will be severely punished from five to fifteen years". Another example is South Sudan, where the law states: "Marital sex is not rape, according to the definition of this section". (Art 247)Conversely, an example of a country where rape law explicitly states marital rape Namibia - Anti-Rape Act (No. 8 of 2000) states: "No marriage or other relationship shall be a precaution against rape cases under this Act."An example of an area where marital rape is a separate offense in Bhutan where 'marital rape' is defined by Article 199 which reads: "The defendant shall be guilty of marital rape, if the defendant has sexual intercourse with his partner consent or against the will of another spouse."

In 1986, in Europe, there was international pressure to criminalize marital rape: The European Parliament's Resolution on Violence Against Women demanded that 1986 be criminalized.This was emphasized by Recommendation Rec (2002) 5 of the Inter-Ministerial Committee on the Protection of Women in the Fight against Violence.(see section 35) This recommendation provides detailed guidelines on how the law on domestic violence, rape, and other forms of violence against women should work. It also provided a definition of violence against women, and provided a list of incomplete examples, including marital rape. Although the approach to the issue of violence against women is very different in European countries, the traditional notion that acts of violence against women are crimes against dignity and morality, not against women's independence, was still widespread in the country. 1990s in many countries. The above recommendation was that member states should "ensure that criminal law provides for any act of violence against a person, particularly physical or sexual violence, including a violation of a person's freedom and integrity physically, mentally and / or sexually, and not only. "(section 34). The approach to sex and other forms of violence against women in some European countries did not reflect the rights of women in other aspects of life (such as public or political life) in those countries: in fact, A 2008 report by Amnesty International described the Danish law on sexual violence as "unconstitutional for international human rights", which led to Denmark eventually changing its sexual offenses law in 2013. (Until 2013, in Denmark "the Penal Code reduced the sentence level or gave the imposition of a full sentence for rape and sexual violence in marriage in certain circumstances and if the perpetrator entered into or continued in marriage with his victim the punishment of rape could be reduced or dismissed"). Cultural and religious values that support women's subjection and inequality are considered essential in addressing the issue of violence against women; but there have been calls for an analysis of cultural norms that allow violence against women to be based on speculative ideology; Mala Htun and S. Laurel Weldon writes that "gender policy is not just one issue but many" and "As Latin American countries are quicker to adopt policies that address violence against women than Nordic countries, one should at least consider the possibility of new integration approaches to further gender policy research." The causes of tolerance - legal or in practice - marital violence are complex; lack of understanding of the concept of consent and coercion due to lack of sex education and public discourse about sex is often cited as the causes of sexual harassment in general; but there has been criticism of the notion that sex education about consent, in itself, is sufficient.

Countries that choose to ratify the Council of Europe Convention on the Prevention and Combating of Violence Against Women and Domestic

Violence, Europe's first legally binding instrument in the field of violence against women.The meeting went into effect in August 2014. In its explanatory report (section 219) it acknowledges the long-standing tradition of tolerance, de jure or de facto, of marital rape and domestic violence:

"A large number of cases established in accordance with this Agreement are usually perpetrated by family members, close associates or others in the immediate victim's social environment. of violence, for example, married or in a relationship. The most common example is marital rape, which for a long time could not be considered rape because of the relationship between the victim and the perpetrator. "

CHAPTER FIVE

LEGAL CHANGES

Countries pre-commissioned for rape include the Soviet Union (1922), Poland (1932), Czechoslovakia (1950), other members of the Communist Bloc, Sweden (1965), and Norway (1971) I Slovenia, a former republic within the federal Yugoslavia, legalized marital rape in 1977. The Supreme Court of Israel has ruled that marital rape is a violation of the 1980 decision, citing law based on the Talmud (at least the 6th century). Crime crime in Australia began with the state of New South Wales in 1981, followed by all other provinces from 1985 to 1992. Several former British colonies followed the same: Canada (1983), New Zealand (1985), and Ireland (1990).

Rape was committed in Austria in 1989 (and in 2004 it was a state case that meant prosecuting the state even without a complaint from the spouse, through procedures such as rape of a stranger). In Switzerland marital rape was a crime in 1992 (and it was a state crime in 2004). In Spain, the Supreme Court ruled in 1992 that sex in marriage must be based on the principle that sex in marriage must be understood in accordance with the principle of free will regarding sexual relations; in doing so agreed to the sentencing of a man convicted of raping his wife in a lower court.

In Europe, Finland banned marriage in 1994. The case of domestic violence in Finland has become a matter of interest and negotiation, because Finland is considered a country where women have the most developed rights in terms of public health and participation in the public sector (jobs, opportunities, etc.). The country has been plagued by international criticism of its approach to violence against women. A 2010 Eurobarometer study on European attitudes toward violence against women showed that the attitudes toward victims were more common in Finland than in other countries: 74 percent of Finns blamed "offensive behavior on women" for violence against women, far higher than in other countries. (For example, many countries believed to be among the most powerful European leaders were less likely to agree with that assertion: 33% in Spain, 46% in Ireland, 47% in Italy). Belgium soon filed a lawsuit against marital rape. In 1979, the Brussels Court of Appeals ruled in favor of the marriage and found that the husband who used extreme violence to force his wife to have sex against his will was guilty of rape. The court's view was that, although the husband had the 'right' to have sex with his wife, he could not use force to seduce her, since Belgian law did not allow people to obtain their rights violently. [62] 63] In 1989 the laws were amended, the definition of rape was expanded, and marital rape began to be treated in the same way as other forms of rape.

In Ireland, the Criminal Law (Rape) Act, 1981 defined rape as "illicit sex" without consent; an attempt to explicitly sanction a married couple's definition was rejected by Fianna Fail's government. Seán Doherty, the Minister of Justice, has suggested that the courts may allow a case of rape in some cases, and that various assault cases may be prosecuted in others. The 1987 Commission of Inquiry into the Law Reform Commission stated, "In the absence of Irish decisions on the topic, the current law cannot be said with great confidence. being, or even, perhaps, where it is considered. "The paperwork to end any divorce" was generally accepted, although some doubts were raised as to whether it might lead to false claims and improper interference in the marital relationship. "The Criminal Justice (Amendment) Act, 1990 deleted the word "illegal" from the 1981 definition. rape, and abolished "any law against which a man could not be guilty of raping his wife". The first two cases were decided in 2006 (when the case was reopened) and in 2016.

In France, in 1990, after a case in which a man abused and raped his wife, the Court of Appeals authorized the prosecution of spouses for rape or sexual assault. In 1992 the Court convicted a man guilty of raping his wife, stating that the consideration of whether a couple should allow sexual acts to take place in a marriage is only valid if the contrary is not confirmed. In 1994, Act 94-89 criminalized marital rape; the second law, passed 4 April 2006, made the rape of partners (including unmarried relationships, marriages, and civil unions) more serious in prosecuting rape.

Germany banned marital rape in 1997, which is more recent than in other developed countries. Women ministers and women's rights activists have been campaigning for more than 25 years. Prior to 1997, the definition of rape was: "Anyone who forces a woman to have sex outside of marriage, or with a third party, forcibly or with threats of life or limb, will be punished with less than two years." imprisonment ". In 1997 there were changes in the law of rape, which expanded the definition, which rendered sexual neutrality, and the abolition of marriage. Blasphemy "(Article 185 of the German Criminal Code) and" Using threats or force to cause a person to suffer. or leave the act "(Nötigung, Section 240 of the German Criminal Code) which carried the lowest sentences and was rarely prosecuted.

Before the new Criminal Code came into effect in 2003, the rape law in Bosnia and Herzegovina also contained a legal release, and it reads: or the body of a person close to him, he will be sentenced to one to ten years in prison. " In Portugal and, prior to 1982, there was a legal release.

Marital rape was committed in Serbia in 2002; prior to that date rape was legally defined as forced sex outside of marriage. This was the case in Hungary until 1997.

In 1994, Judgment No. 223/94 V, 1994, the Luxembourg Court of Appeal affirmed the application of the provisions of the Criminal Code regarding rape in marital rape.

Marital rape was illegal in the Netherlands in 1991. Legislative reforms provided a new definition of rape in 1991, which abolished divorce, and made crime a gender neutral; prior to 1991 the legal definition of rape was to force, violently or intimidate a woman to have sex outside of marriage.

In Italy the law of rape, the violenza carnale ('physical violence', as it was called) did not contain a legal release, but, as elsewhere, was perceived as invalid in the context of marriage. Although Italy has a reputation for traditional male domination of men, it was too early to acknowledge that rape law included forced sex in marriage: 1976 Sentenza n. 12857 del 1976, the Supreme Court ruled that "a spouse who coerces another spouse with carnal knowledge through violent acts or threats commits physical violence" ("committing the crime of sexual violence to the corporate and socially incorrect).".

Cyprus made marital rape a crime in 1994. Marital rape was illegal in Northern Macedonia in 1996. In Croatia marital rape was committed in 1998.

In 2006, Greece enacted Law 3500/2006, entitled "Combating Domestic Violence", punishing marital rape. He took office on October 24, 2006. The law also prohibits many other forms of marital violence and cohabitation, as well as various other forms of violence against women.

Liechtenstein committed illegal marital rape in 2001.

In South America, Colombia made marital rape a crime in 1996, and a crime in Chile.

Thailand outlawed marital rape in 2007. New changes were made amid intense conflicts and opposition from many. Another opponent of the law was the legal expert Taweekiet Meenakanit who expressed his opposition to the changes in the law. He also opposed the criminalization of rape. Meenakanit argued that allowing a husband to open up to his wife for rape was "out of the ordinary" and that wives refuse to divorce or imprison their husbands because most Thai women rely on their husbands.

Papua New Guinea criminalized marital rape in 2003. Namibia outlawed marital rape in 2000.

Section 375 of the Indian Penal Code (IPC) treats forced sexual intercourse in marriages only as a crime when the wife is under 15 years of age. Thus, marital rape is not a crime under the IPC. Victims of marital rape must seek assistance under the Protection of Women from Domestic Violence Act 2005 (PWDVA). PWDVA, which came into effect in 2006, condemns marital rape. However, it only provides a public solution to the case. [106] In February 2022, Smriti Irani (Minister for the Development of Women and Children) informed parliament that "the Indian government has begun a process of fully amending criminal law through consultation" to answer questions on marital rape, ensuring that certain provisions are made. by committing the crime of rape in a marriage.

Recent countries that have made marital rape criminal include Zimbabwe (2001), Turkey (2005), Cambodia (2005), Liberia (2006), Nepal (2006), Mauritius (2007), Ghana (2007), Malaysia (2007), Thailand (2007), Rwanda (2009), Suriname (2009) , Nicaragua (2012), Sierra Leone (2012), South Korea (2013), Bolivia (2013), Samoa (2013), Tonga (1999/2013). Human rights activists have criticized various countries for failing to prosecute marital rape in the first place. South Africa, which committed a crime in 1993, was first convicted of marital rape in 2012.

United States

A common definition of rape in the United States is the sexual harassment of a man and a "woman who is not his wife", making it clear that these laws do not apply to married couples. The Model Penal Code of 1962 was again released on marital rape, stating:

A man who has sex with a woman who is not his wife is guilty of rape if:

....

Changes to rape laws in the United States began in the mid-1970's by making marital rape a criminal offense. The earlier laws of the 1970's often stipulated that a husband and wife could no longer live together in order to file charges of marital rape. The case in the United States that first challenged this settlement clause was Oregon v. Rideout 1978. Although the husband was acquitted of raping his wife, it prompted a movement toward change. In 1993 marital rape was a crime in all 50 states. Nevertheless, during the 1990's, many states continued to distinguish between the view that marital rape and marital rape were viewed and handled. Laws continue to change and emerge, with many provinces changing their laws in the 21st century. But there are still states, such as South Carolina, where rape of a married or unmarried person is treated very differently under the law.

During the 1990's, many states distinguished between the practice of marital rape and the subsequent marital rape. This difference was reflected in the short-term penalties, whether the violence was used or not, and the permissive reporting periods. (Bergen, 1996; Russell, 1990). Laws have continued to change and change, with many states changing their laws in the 21st century, to make marital rape laws more relevant to extraordinary rapes, but even today there are still differences in some states. With the removal, in 2005, of the requirement for a high level of violence in Tennessee law, now allowing marital rape in Tennessee to be treated like any other form of rape, South Carolina remains a form of rape. only the US region has a law that requires extreme force / violence (force or violence used or threatened should be a "high and violent environment").

In many provinces criminal activity has taken place by abolishing exemptions from ordinary rape law, or by courts overturning such exemptions as unconstitutional.Some states have committed a separate crime of rape. California, for example, has various criminal charges of rape (Article 261) and rape of a spouse (Article 262).

ENGLAND AND WALES

Although the issue of marital rape was highlighted in the 19th century by women's rights activists, it was also repulsed by such thinkers as John Stuart Mill and Bertrand Russell (see paragraph 1 'Criticism of Women in the 19th Century), it did not end there until the 1970's. the issue was raised at the political level. In the late 1970's, the Sexual Offenses (Amendment) Act of 1976 was enacted, which provided the first official definition of rape (prior to this rape was defined by general law). The Criminal Law Revision Committee in its 1984 report on sexual crimes dismissed the notion that rape cases should extend to marital relations; the following writing:

"Most of us ... believe that rape cannot be taken for granted. sex always before the act in question and, because sexual intercourse may involve a certain degree of compromise, sometimes you may only agree with some hesitation. and that the 'unique' case and the 'grave' described at the outset. "Where the husband goes.

The Committee also expressed broad views on domestic violence as "Violence occurs in some marriages but women do not always wish the marriage bond to be terminated" and emphasized the fact that domestic incidents without physical harm will usually be outside the scope of the Act: "Some of us think criminal law should not enter. in marital relationships between spouses - especially the marriage bed - except where the injury occurs, where other charges can be filed."

Five years later, in Scotland, the Supreme Court of Justice took a different view, ending marital insecurity, in the case of S. v. H.M. Advocate, 1989. The same thing happened in England and Wales in 1991, in R v R (see below). Shortly afterwards, in Australia, at the end of 1991, in R v L, the Australian Supreme Court issued a similar ruling, ruling that if liberation from common law had been a part of Australian law, it was no longer (by. Then provinces and territories).many Australians had completed their legal release).

It ends with the release

A West Midlands police poster 2012 against sexual violence, calling marriage 'no excuse'

Release from marital rape was first discussed in 1736 in Matthew Hale's book A History of the Pleas of the Crown (see above). It was abolished in England and Wales in 1991 by the House of Commons Appeals Committee, in the case of R v R, which was the first time that the liberation of marriage rights was appealed to the end. House of Lords, and has followed three cases since 1988 in which the release of marital rights was maintained. The leading verdict, unanimously, was given by Lord Keith of Kinkel. He argued that the controversy in the lower courts to prevent the use of marital liberation was an indication of the folly of the law, and he was arrested, agreeing with Scottish earlier decisions and the Court of Appeal in R v R, stating that " it was a myth of general law "which had never been a true law of English law. R's complaint was dismissed, and he was convicted of raping his wife.

The first attempt to prosecute a husband for raping his wife was R v Clarke (1949). Rather than attempting to contradict Hale's views, the court ruled that consent in the case had been revoked by a court order not to cohabit. It was the first time in many cases that the courts had found reasons not to grant release, especially R v O'Brien (1974) R v Roberts (1986) (the existence of a valid divorce agreement).

There are at least four recorded cases of a husband who successfully relied on liberation in England and Wales. The first was R v Miller (1954), in which it was alleged that the wife did not formally withdraw her consent despite filing for divorce. R v Kowalski (1988) was followed by R v Sharples (1990), and R v J (1991), a decision that was issued after the first State Court decision in R v R but before the decision. of the House of Lords which would complete the release. In Miller, Kowalski and R v J husbands instead were convicted of assault. The case of R and Kowalski involved, among other things, an incident of oral sex without consent. As a result, the husband was convicted of abuse, as the court ruled that his wife's "consensual consent" for marriage should extend to sexual intercourse, not to other acts such as fellatio. [151] (At the time the 'rape' case was only about sex.) In R v Sharples (1990) there were allegations that the husband raped his wife in 1989. Allegations of rape, the judge refused to accept that rape was legal, concluding that the family protection order did not revoke the wife's consent, declaring that: "

Aftermath

By 1991, when the release was lifted, the Legal Commission in its 1990 Working Paper had already endorsed the abolition of the release, a view expressed in their Final Report published in 1992; and international travel in this way was now commonplace. Therefore, the outcome of the R v R case was accepted. But, although the removal of the release itself was not controversial, the manner in which this was done; as the change was not made by a standard legal modification. SW v UK and CR v UK cases come from responding to R v R; in which the applicants (convicted of rape and attempted rape of women) appealed to the European Court of Human Rights (ECHR) claiming that their conviction was a violation of the law following the violation of Article 7 of the European Convention on Human Rights. They said at the time of the rape there was a common law of release, so their condemnation was post facto. Their case was unsuccessful, as their arguments were rejected by the European Court of Human Rights, which ruled that criminalizing marital rape was a forerunner of criminal law because of the changing social norms; and that Section 7 does not preclude a gradual change in the judgment of the case, provided that the outcome is consistent with the context of the case and can be reasonably predicted.

The new definition of 'rape' was established in 1994 by section 142 of the Criminal Justice and Social Planning Act, 1994, providing a comprehensive definition of anal sex; and a broader definition was established by the Sexual Offenses Act of 2003, which includes oral sex. The rape law never — and never since the dissolution of a marriage in 1991 — provides for any alternative punishment based on the relationship between the parties. However, in 1993, in R v W 1993 14 Cr App R (S) 256, a court ruled: "It should not be assumed that a separate and lower degree automatically applies to the rape of a woman by her husband. the circumstances of the case. When the parties are living together and the man persists in having sex against his wife's wishes but without violence or threats this may reduce the sentence. When the behavior is bad and involves threats or violence the relationship will not be worth it."

NORTHERN IRELAND

During the time of R v R (see "England and Wales" above), rape in Northern Ireland was a common law offense. Northern Ireland common law is similar to that of England and Wales, and in part comes from the same sources; therefore any (suspected) exemption from its rape law was also overturned by R v R. In March 2000, a Belfast man was convicted of raping his wife, in the first case of its kind in Northern Ireland.

Until 28 July 2003, rape in Northern Ireland remained a common law that could only be committed by a man against a woman only as in the case of female genital mutilation. Between 28 July 2003 and 2 February 2009 rape was defined by the Criminal Justice (Northern Ireland) Order 2003 as "any sexual act without the consent of a man", but the common law case continued to exist, as well as oral sex. he sat outside. On 2 February 2009 the Order of Sexual Offenses (Northern Ireland) Order 2008 came into force, abolished the common law of rape, and provided a definition of rape similar to that of the Sexual Offenses Act of 2003 in England and Wales. The Public Prosecution Service of Northern Ireland has the same policy on marital rape as other forms of rape; states in its policy on Prosecuting Prosecution Policy: "The policy applies to all forms of rape, including marital and sexual assault, rape of a relative and rape of a stranger, both male and female victims".

AUSTRALIA

In Australia, the insecurity of marital rape was removed from all provinces and territories, either by law or by law, between the late 1970s and early 1990s. Previously, exemptions from marital rape were based on the common English law of rape, commonly understood as "physical knowledge", outside of marriage, by a woman who did not want to. The definition of common law of rape continued to apply in some jurisdictions, with some writing a definition, in each case involving divorce. In Queensland, for example, the principle stated: "Anyone who has physical knowledge of a woman or a girl, not his wife, without her consent, or consent, if the consent is obtained by force, or by threats or intimidation of any kind, or by fear of physical harm, or by false statements. or fraud regarding the nature of the act, or, in the case of a married woman, by making herself her husband, guilty, is called rape."

The first Australian country to experience marital rape was South Australia, under the ongoing plans of Prime Minister Don Dunstan, which in 1976 gradually released. Section 73 of the Consolidation Act Amendment Act of 1976 (SA) reads: "No person shall, on the ground that he is married to another person, be deemed to have consented to have sexual relations with that person". However, laws did not limit marriage equality to unmarried rape; the law required violence or other serious circumstances, in order for a sexual act to be a rape.

The first Australian authority to abolish divorce was New South Wales in 1981. Western Australia, Victoria, and ACT did the same in 1985; and Tasmania in 1987. Negotiations for marital rape had already taken place in Queensland in the late 1970s,but it was not until 1989 that liberation was abolished and the Northern Territory did the same in 1994. In 1991, in the case of R v L, the Australian Supreme Court ruled that "if there is a general law"

India

In India there are no legal provisions relating to marital rape and they are required by the commission to make laws that will bring you to the crime scene.

CHAPTER SIX

MARRIAGE AFTER RAPE

In various cultures, a marriage after the rape of an unmarried woman is traditionally considered a "decision" of the rape, that is, a "remarriage". In some lands, simply promising to marry a rapist is enough to free the perpetrator from criminal prosecution. Although laws against felony criminal mischief for marrying a victim of rape are often associated with the Middle East,such laws were common throughout the world until the second half of the 20th century. By the end of 1997, for example, 14 Latin American countries had such laws, even though most of these countries have now repealed them.

Whether women are forced to marry their rapist, or a marriage is dissolved before the violence begins, many victims remain in a relationship of perpetual violence. While there are many reasons why victims of marital rape remain in their marriages, one important reason is that divorce can be difficult to obtain and / or discriminated against (Kwiatowski, 70). Contrary to tradition, one of the barriers that keep victims in their marriages shame is the guilt and guilt they feel about marital rape (Bergen, 2016), or common sexual barriers (Kwiatkowski, 2016) (Torres, 2016). Finally, some victims do not include their abuse as marital rape in order to reduce the violence they tolerate. This is used as a form of self-defense so that they can continue to tolerate their abuse (Menjívar, 2016).

In the case of forced marriage with a child

Compulsory marriages and child marriage are widespread in many parts of the world, especially in parts of Asia and Africa. Compulsory marriage is a marriage in which one or both partners marry without their expressly granted consent; while child marriage is a marriage in which one or both spouses are younger than 18. These types of marriages are associated with higher levels of domestic violence, including marital rape. These types of marriages are more common in traditional societies that do not have laws against sexual abuse in marriage, and where it is very difficult to leave the marriage. Incidents occurring in some of these countries (such as Yemen) have received worldwide attention. According to the World Health Organization, under the heading "Types of sexual violence", (page 156):

"Marriage is often used to justify forms of violence against women. The practice of marrying young children, especially girls, is found in many parts of the world. or she knows nothing about sex before marriage. "

Other forced marriages took place in Guatemala (also called robadas) and in Mexico (called rapto). Robadas refers to "... abduction, where women are' taken 'during courtship, sometimes voluntarily but sometimes by force, by someone who wants to start a marital relationship with them" (Menjívar, 2016). Rapto means "... sexual abduction or lust or marriage" (Bovarnik, 2007). After being abducted, marriage is often encouraged to maintain the dignity of the family (Bovarnik, 2007).

In these types of forced marriages, the marital bond begins with a man's strong sense of control over the woman, combined with the realization that the wife is the property of her husband (Menjívar, 2016). This foundation for marriage had a direct impact on sexual violence in marriage. Referring to the practice of robadas, Cecilia Menjívar (2016) writes, "... unions that begin in rooda violence can continue to breed violence, harassment, and mistreatment in the organization." In addition, women who are victims of robadas often face shame and suspicion, despite the actions often initiated by male perpetrators (Menjívar, 2016). Women are accused of disobeying their parents or resisting their captors strong enough (Menjívar, 2016). The idea of blaming this woman also comes up when it comes to rapport in rural Mexico. Silvie Bovarnik (2007) writes, "In many cases, men and women alike view the error of responsibility in women's conduct because of the common perceptions of women as 'pillars of honor.' Many of these women, who were given little choice in their marriage, were left to live with their abusers.

CHAPTER SEVEN

PRELEVANCE

According to a study cited by Gary F. Kelly (2011), 9% of victims of female genital mutilation are raped by their spouse.

Marital rape is difficult to detect, especially outside the Western world. Talking about sex in many cultures is illegal. One problem with marital rape studies is that the Western concept of confession is not understood in many parts of the world. Because so many societies work on social norms that create a double standard of sexual behavior — marital sex that is considered to be irrevocable, and marital discord, which seems unfair (or illegal / illegal). Permission issues are not well understood, especially by young women (often young girls who do not fully understand sexual rights). For example, in an interview with a World Health Organization study, a Bangladeshi woman who described her husband's physical abuse as being forced to have sex said: "I thought that this was normal. This is how a man behaves. The study, however, linked specific regions with high levels of violence, including sexual violence, against women by their partners / partners. An example of that is Ethiopia.

The prevalence of marital rape depends largely on the legal, national, and cultural context. In 1999, the World Health Organization conducted a study of violence against women in Tajikistan, surveying 900 women over the age of 14 in three states and found that 47% of married women reported being forced to have sex with their husbands. In Turkey 35.6 percent of women have been raped in marriage and 16.3% more often.

The first Western study attempting to investigate marital rape was the Join Seites' unpublished study of the spring of 1975. Seites sent questions to 40 rape crisis centers from a list compiled by the Center for Women Policy Studies (Washington, DC). 16 institutions completed a questionnaire with a response rate of 40%. Of the 3,709 reported calls related to rape and attempted rape received by 16 institutions, 12 were reporting marital rape

(0.3%). Because rape crisis centers have not always recorded the caller's relationship, even if the 12 reported calls fully represent the number of spouses, it cannot be ascertained.

In 1982 Diana E. H. Russell, a writer and activist for women's rights, conducted a small study on marital rape. Her study surveyed a total of 930 women in San Francisco, California (50% of non-respondents, English-speaking Asian women were not included in the list of unfaithful respondents), 644 of whom were married, divorced, or self-identified. as a husband even though you are not married. Six of these women (1%) surveyed had been raped by their ex-husbands, ex-husbands, or ex-husbands. Their interlocutors, however, identified 74 (12%) of these women as rape victims. Of the 286 single women in the sample, 228 (80%) were identified by their interviewees as rape. Russell found that when recurring rapes as separated by interviewers, husbands or ex-husbands, during the entire marriage were included, this accounted for 38% of all rape cases, compared with the remaining 62 percent. in single cases.

David Finkelhor and Kersti Yllo published a study in 1985 on marital rape that used a sample of a scientifically selected site from the Boston metropolitan area of 323 married or married women with a child living with them within six years. and fourteen. Studies have found that in married women the occurrence of sexual intercourse by using physical force or your threat is 3%.

In 1994, Patricia Easteal, then a Senior Criminologist at the Australian Institute of Criminology, published the results of a study on sexual harassment in many places. Respondents were all victims of many forms of sexual harassment. In the small sample of victims, 10.4% were raped by real husbands or husbands, while another 2.3% were raped by divorced husbands.

In 2002 Basile published a study aimed at addressing the shortage of opportunities in the country to date that measured the deepest sexual oppression faced by married women. Data were collected from a 1997 national survey by random telephone survey of 1,108 inhabitants of the U.S. continent. of persons 18 years of age or older. The survey had a response rate of 50%. Of the 1,108 respondents, 506 men were not included in any survey regarding unwanted sexual feelings, leaving 602 (54%) of women who responded to the study. 398 women (66%) reported abstinence (their marital status is not provided), and 204 women (34%) responded by having unwanted sex after being forced into a certain level of sex; forms of sexual coercion included receiving a 'gift', 'a delicious dinner', 'rubbing the back', 'kissing', etc. with threatened and forced physical injuries. In this group, a small sample of 120 (59%) were married, of which 9% of them responded that they were underweight.

•25•

CHAPTER EIGHT

PHYSICAL AND PSYCHOLOGICAL INJURIES

Rape of a spouse, partner, or ex-partner is often associated with physical violence. A nine-nation study within the European Union found that current or former partners were the perpetrators of all 25% sexual assault, and that violence was more frequent in attacks by ex-partners (50% of the time) and partners (40%) than beatings by strangers or acquaintances out (25%).

Proving the effects of marital rape in the study is problematic as it is almost impossible to find a large enough sample of study partners who have experienced sexual violence but who have never been abused by their partners. Marital rape can spread sexually transmitted diseases and HIV, adversely affecting the victim's physical and mental health. In sub-Saharan countries with a high rate of HIV transmission, such as Lesotho, co-occurrence and marital rape cases increase the spread of HIV.

Although rape of a stranger is very traumatic, it is usually a one-time event and is clearly understood as rape. In the case of rape by a partner or long-term sexual partner, the history of the relationship affects the victim's reaction. There are studies that show that marital rape can be more devastating emotionally and physically than being raped by a stranger.Marital rape can happen as part of an abusive relationship. Harassment as a result of rape adds to the consequences of other abusive acts or abusive and degrading speech. Moreover, marital rape is rarely a one-off event, but it is a recurring one if not always. Whether it occurs once or is part of a fixed form of domestic violence, the trauma from rape has long-term consequences for victims whether the assault is prosecuted or not.

Unlike other forms of rape, where the victim is able to withdraw from the rapist's company and never reunite with him, in the case of marital rape the victim usually has no choice but to continue living with his or her partner: in many marriages. Researchers Finkelhor and Yllö observed in their 1985 study of the metropolitan area of Boston:

"If a woman is raped by a stranger, she must live with a horrible memory. If she is raped by her husband, she should stay with the rapist."

CHAPTER NINE

RELATIONSHIPS WITH OTHER FORMS OF MARITAL VIOLENCE

History (and today in places where it still works) the insecurity of men to have sexual relations with their wives without consent was not the end of marital protection against abuse; insecurity in the use of violence was common (and still in some countries) —a way of a husband's right to apply "limited punishment" to a 'disobedient' wife. In the US, many provinces, especially the Southern ones, maintained this immunity until the middle of the 19th century. For example, in 1824, in the case of Calvin Bradley v. State, the Mississippi Supreme Court upholds this right of the husband; we rule as follows:

"Family disputes and disagreements will not be investigated in the national courts, without prejudice to the conduct of the victims. all forms of misconduct, other than criminal charges, which result in injury and humiliation to all parties involved. "

Although by the end of the 19th century, the courts had unanimously agreed that husbands no longer had the right to "punish" their wives, a policy of public policy was set aside to prevent so-called 'bad enough' cases to intervene. In 1874, the North Carolina Supreme Court ruled:

"We may think that the old doctrine, that a husband has the right to beat his wife, as long as he uses a button larger than six, is not a law in North Carolina.

But on the basis of public policy, - in order to maintain the sanctity of civil society, courts will not hear trivial complaints.

If there is no lasting harm done, or hatred, cruelty or dangerous violence shown by the husband, it is better to close the curtain, close the public eye, and leave the victims to forget and forgive.

There is no standard rule, but each case must be based on the circumstances surrounding us. "

Today, husbands continue to face persecution in the face of physical abuse in other countries. In Iraq, for example, husbands have the legal right to "punish" their wives. The criminal code states that there is no crime if the act was committed while exercising a legal right. Examples of legal rights include: "Punishment of the wife by her husband, punishment by parents and teachers of children under their control within certain limits set by law or tradition". In 2010, the United Arab Emirates Supreme Court ruled that a man has the right to punish his wife and children as long as he does not leave his mark.

CHAPTER TEN

VIOLENCE AGAINST A WOMAN

Although most studies focus on women as victims of marital rape, men also face marital rape. A small study is available that focuses on the specific nature of an unacceptable sexual relationship between a man and a woman, but evidence shows that 13% -16% of men are victims of sexual assault or living together (Tjaden and Thoennes, 2000). Studies by Morse (1995), Straus (1977-1978), and Straus and Gelles (1985) suggest that men and women have almost the same levels of sexual harassment of a spouse or roommate (Tjaden and Thoennes, 2000). One study looking at a lifelong experience of marital and cohabiting violence found almost equal levels of violence between men and women (Tjaden and Thoennes, 2000). However, these figures convey a major theme of partner violence and do not reflect marital rape rates. failed confirmation - see discussion

<u>SUPPORTING FEATURES</u>

Legal

Legally, governments have a direct bearing on marital rape cases. The region "... is involved in the interpretation, monitoring, and commissioning of appropriate conduct" (Torres, 2016). This can play a role in committing a crime or not making it a crime to rape a marriage and therefore take appropriate action. Catharine MacKinnon argues that rape laws in male-dominated societies exist to regulate women's access to men's views, not to protect women's right to freely decide whether or not to have sex. Whatever the reason for such laws, even when the laws of the land criminalize marital infidelity, government agencies continue to enforce them. For example, although marital rape has been criminalized throughout the United States, the early 1980's and 1990's dealt with marital rape differently from single rape, and in some states this is still the case today (see marital rape) . As these rules show, marital rape is considered to be less blameworthy in some way than extramarital affairs (Bergen, 2016). Even when marital rape is successfully prosecuted, courts often issue short sentences - even if the law itself does not stipulate - based on the perception that sexual harassment is less serious in a marriage. Following this same understanding, British courts often impose lower marital rape sentences than other rape cases because they are believed to cause less harm to the victim (Mandal, 2014).

Police departments are another government agency that treats domestic violence differently than other forms of violence. Police often refer to domestic violence calls as less important, less responsive, and more likely to focus on aggression rather than on the perpetrator's violent acts (Schelong, 1994). Also, they often act as mediators in this situation because they may feel that domestic violence is a family affair and therefore not their business (Schelong, 1994).

Although there are many influences on public institutions, marital rape is often based on traditional beliefs. According to Catharine MacKinnon and Andrea Dworkin, the issue of sexual violence, including marriage, is not a political issue - it is a left-wing issue compared to the right-wing - but part of the traditional culture, "The Left and Right have always had differing views on rape; of women who have been raped.

Cultural Unrecognizable

In many cultures, perceptions of marital rape appear to be often forced and contradict the belief that such matters should be handled in private and not by the government (Smith, 2016). In some cases, especially in India, members of the public have spoken out publicly that marital rape cannot be recognized in their culture. The Minister of Home Affairs of India, Haribhai Parthibhai Chaudhary, stated in April 2015, "The concept of marital rape, as understood internationally, cannot be properly applied in the Indian context due to various factors, including educational levels, illiteracy, poverty., Multiculturalism and values. social, religious beliefs, [and] the public perception of marriage as a sacrament "(Torres, 2016). In many other countries, the concept of marital rape itself is oxymoron (Smith, 2016). Women in these cultures in particular "... share the traditional notion that marital rape is a conditional conflict ..." while men at the same time "... see women's sexual consent in marriage as something that is considered normal ..." and as a result "... reject it and the concept of marital rape "(Smith, 2016).

The act of forcing sex against a woman's will is often not known as bad, so it is difficult to try to stop the practice, "Usually, men who force a partner to perform a sexual act believe their actions are legal because they are married to a woman." (WHO, p. 149). The idea that sex in marriage is 'legal' and therefore not legal even if it is compulsory, in some parts of the world is fueled by the practice of lobola: your payment is considered to earn a man's right to have sex and to reproduce. to control his wife. UN Women commended the abolition of bribery, and stated: "The law should state that the perpetrator of domestic violence, including marital rape, cannot use the fact that he paid lobola as protection against domestic violence. charge. (page 25)

Young women from various parts of South Asia explained in a study that even if they felt uncomfortable and did not want to have sex, they would accept their husbands' wishes and submit to them, fearing that otherwise they would be beaten. [196] In many developing countries it is believed — both men and women — that a man has the right to have sex whenever he wants it, and that if his wife refuses, he has the right to exercise his authority. These women, most of whom are illiterate or highly illiterate, married at a very young age (in Bangladesh, for example, according to 2005 statistics, 45% of women then between the ages of 25-29 were married by the age of 15. and relied on their husbands for the rest of their lives. This situation leaves women with very little sexual independence. The idea that women are capable of sexual independence and therefore the ability to grant or withdraw consent is not universally understood. Gabriella Torres writes, "The degree to which women and men view themselves as socially incapable of having the ability to make decisions and suffer the consequences varies from culture to culture" (Torres, 2016). are not considered independent, they are not in a position to reject sex: they have to choose between unwanted sex and being subjected to violence; or between unwanted sex and the abandonment of their husbands and end up living in abject poverty.

According to Sheila Jeffreys, in the West, the notion of "sexual liberties" has exacerbated the problem of male sexual empowerment, leading women to submit to sex not only because of physical force or illegal threat, but also because of social pressure: and working in marriages and relationships are often less obvious. These forces include the major sex industry, sex medicine, sex counseling books, all of which make women feel guilty and unworthy of any unwillingness to fulfill a man's sexual desires."

Prohibition of rape serves other purposes, such as the protection of the rights of male or female relatives, the enforcement of religious laws against sex outside of marriage, or the preservation of a woman's dignity and dignity in society. Under such ideas it is difficult to accept the concept of marital rape. Richard A. Posner writes, "Traditionally, rape was a crime of depriving a father or husband of important property - the purity of his wife or the virginity of his daughter". In many countries of the world, including Morocco, Algeria, Tunisia, Jordan, the severity of the legal penalty for rape depends on the victim's virginity. Rhonda Copleon writes, "When rape is considered a crime against dignity, respect for women is doubtful and virginity or innocence is often the first condition.

The way marriage are arranged

In many lands, marriages are arranged, with the goal of producing offspring, property, and strengthening family ties, which often include lobola or lobola. In such cases, weddings are arranged in advance as a matter of family and family relationships. In some cultures, a person's refusal to accept an arranged marriage is often the result of honorable death, for the family that prepares for marriage risks the risk of humiliation if the marriage does not proceed. Although laws against bribery exist in many lands, men continue to demand lobola in marriage, especially in rural areas where the law is weak. In Bangladesh, demand for lobola in marriage is linked to increased sexual violence. A woman who is trying to get a divorce or divorce without the consent of her extended husband / family can be the cause of honorable murder. In cultures where marriages are arranged and property is often traded between families, a woman's desire for divorce is often viewed as an insult to men who negotiate an agreement.

However, the fact that people in developing lands are increasingly selective in their choice of marriage partners — a view of the West is far from ideal — does not really improve the situation. These types of marriages, especially in southeastern Nigeria, place women in a very difficult position: if a person chooses to marry based on love against his or her family desires, admitting violence in a relationship is shameful because it means acknowledging that one has made the wrong decision (Smith, 2016).

CHAPTER ELEVEN

RELIGION

Christianity

Most Western lands have been greatly influenced by the Judeo-Christian Bible. The paradisaic story of the man and woman in Genesis lays the foundation for a marriage:

"So God created man in his own image, in the image of God created he him; he created him in God's image; male and female he created them. " "Therefore shall a man leave his father and his mother, and shall cleave unto his wife: and they shall be one flesh".

This doctrine is repeated in the Gospels by Jesus, but with a further conclusion "therefore they are no longer two, but one flesh."The same doctrine is repeated in Scripture in the writings of the apostle Paul.

It is also made clear by the apostle Paul, who says that no partner should deny his or her sexual orientation:

"The wife does not have authority over her own body, but the husband does. Likewise also the husband doesn't have authority over his own body, but the wife. Do not deprive one another except with consent for a time, that you may give yourselves to fasting and prayer; and meet again.

In each group's decision to determine how this biblical principle — to deny marital relations — was to be fulfilled was compiled a list of church books in 280 AD by St. Dionysian of Alexandria: "Individuals and couples should be the judges themselves." by the public courts.

The Christian religion teaches that premarital sex is fornication, and sexual relations between unmarried individuals are adultery, both of which are sinful, whereas sexual intimacy within marriage is the practice. The concept of 'marital rights' is intended to prevent sin (adultery and temptation) and to enable us to reproduce.

The above is interpreted by some religious people as making marital rape impossible. However, not all religious people share that view.

In addition, Pentecostal Christianity sets the gender expectations of married people that "... they have restored the patriarchal covenant ..." where "... women acknowledge men's authority for certain forms of support" (Smith, 2016). Men are expected to support the family, and in return, wives are to submit to the authority of their husbands (Smith, 2016). Finally, this "... reinforces some of the gender inequalities that contribute to intimate partner violence from the outset" (Smith, 2016).

In contrast, Pope Paul VI in his 1968 encyclical book Humanae vitae wrote that "Men rightly recognize that a marital act imposed on one's partner without regard for one's status or personal and intellectual preferences in the matter, is not a true act of love. morality in its application especially in the intimate relationship of man and woman. "This doctrine, which has recently been confirmed by Pope Francis, and has been interpreted by Bertrand de Margerie as condemning" marital rape ", as well as the general use of force in marriage.

Islam

Gender exception

Another factor that supports the role of women is responsibility and what they understand as their "job". For example, "Vietnamese women are expected to provide for their families, especially their children, including, for some, by acknowledging the sexual needs of their husbands" (Kwiatkowski, 2016). Their "job" is to maintain family harmony and happiness (Kwiatkowski, 2016). In Guatemala, marital violence is so prevalent that women believe that this is 'the way things are' and that it is simply their role as women to tolerate violence (Menjívar, 2016). This "... general abuse ... is based on the perpetuation of coercive power which results in the mistreatment of women not only in the home but also in the community, region and society as a whole" (Menjívar, 2016). Moreover, because many of these women believe that having sex is their job, they do not see their experience as marital rape (Bergen, 2016). However, "... women who have engaged in forced sex in marriage understand this experience as abuse or violation", they may not see it as marital rape (Torres, 2016). Violence is deeply rooted in many cultures and has become a way of life, and women are left believing that they must learn to tolerate it (Menjívar, 2016).

Men, on the other hand, are influenced by what they expect of their manhood. In Africa, these expectations include being a husband, father, and head of household that requires men to provide food, shelter and protection

(Smith, 2016). Along with this "... the obligation to be a provider comes with the paternal privilege and authority" (Smith, 2016). As a result, it is common for a man to see his wife challenge his authority which leads to violence (Smith, 2016).

In the United States, masculinity is understood to be consistent despite the changes in daily life (Connell, 45). It is understood as a comparison of femininity, and especially, against femininity: masculinity is as high as femininity is submissive (Connell). Thus, masculinity is associated with anger in such a way that scholars say that violence is a way for men to express their masculinity (Umberson et al., 2003). Another expectation of masculinity is that men should not express their feelings (Umberson et al., 2003). Instead, as Robert Connell argues, the "male prototype" is a strong and resilient man who seems to be able to control his mood and emotions (Umberson et al., 2003). This sense of control in Western masculinity has a direct impact on domestic violence. Scholars argue that some men resort to violence to regain this sense of control when lost (Umberson et al., 2003).

However, not all men agree to expect violent manhood. In fact, most men are, in general, non-violent (Umberson et al., 2003). For those who are violent, masculinity seems to play a role in their violence. Studies show that "violence is more common among men who experience differences between their personal circumstances and their emotions" (Umberson et al., 2003). Clearly, there seems to be a link between a man's expectation to suppress or suppress his emotions, and a man's tendency to be violent (Umberson et al., 2003).

CHAPTER TWELVE

UNIVERSAL LIVING EXPERIENCE

Although marital rape may not always be so defined in different cultures, there is a full understanding of the abuse that comes with rape. Yllö & Torres (2016) argues that "... marital rape is often perpetrated in all cultures as a socially recognized violation — understood as preventing women in such cultural contexts from wishing for a better human life." Part of this violation of the idea is that the victim did not give consent, yet, historically still, consent is not always linked to marital sex. (Yllö and Torres, 2016). In the United States, a woman's personality, and therefore her consent, began only with the suffragist movement that sought to achieve women's equality (Yllö & Torres, 2016). Globally, many cultures do not require a woman's consent to marriage because procreation is the root of such an alliance (Yllö & Torres, 2016). In addition, some women are forced to marry when her consent is not considered or required (Yllö & Torres, 2016). Despite these cultural differences, "women in all cultures experience marital abuse — even if the manner in which such abuse occurs and is understood varies from culture to culture" (Yllö & Torres, 2016).

CHAPTER THIRTEEN

PROBLEMS IN PROSECUTING MARITAL RAPE

Being made a criminal offender in marriage does not mean that these rules apply. Lack of public awareness, as well as skepticism or direct refusal of authorities to prosecute is commonplace all over the world. In Ireland, for example, when marital rape was illegal in 1990, in 2016 only two people were convicted of marital rape. Additionally, sexual practices that place wives in subordinate positions make it difficult for women to view their spouse's rape as insignificant or to feel confident that the law will be enforced.

There are, and still are, both current and historical problems with the persecution of married rapists. One author concludes that the great king among them has been the skepticism of various legal systems to see it as a crime at all. For example, in the United Kingdom, rape of a spouse was recognized by a 1991 House of Lords resolution known as R v R (1991 All ER 481).

Another problem arises from existing social norms. Therefore, if social norms do not view marital rape as a justification for violating social norms, marital rape laws are less likely to result in effective prosecution. In Mali, for example, it is considered unthinkable for a woman to reject her husband's sexual interests; far from being considered an act of violence against a wife, marital rape is considered an incident that angered a woman who refused to perform her duties: for example one survey found that 74% of Mali women say that a man has the right to marry. beating his wife if she refuses to have sex with him.

Another problem is that in some lands where marital rape is illegal, most people are not aware of it. In some parts of the world, marital rape laws are relatively new and relatively uncommon, so some people do not even realize it. Alternatively, traditional marriage customs may be more deeply rooted in the human conscience. So a large percentage of people may not think that in any modern theories about sex, it is irritating to force a spouse to have sex is wrong, and a little illegal. For example, a report by Amnesty International showed that although marital rape is illegal in Hungary, in a public survey of nearly 1,200 people in 2006, a total of 62% were unaware that marital rape was a punishable crime: more than 41% of men and women almost 56% thought it could be punished as a crime in Hungarian law, and about 12% did not know.In Hong Kong, in 2003, 16 months after the rape was committed, a survey showed that 40% of women were unaware that it was illegal. A 2010 study in South Africa, (where marital rape was illegal in 1993), showed that only 55% of respondents agreed with the statement "I think it is possible for a woman to be raped by her husband".

Although in recent years some African countries have enacted laws prohibiting marital rape, in many parts of the continent, sex outside of marriage is not a crime. A 2003 report by Human Rights Watch stated: "With the exception of a few in Africa, marital rape is not considered a crime, and domestic violence is considered a right for married men." Percentage of women aged 15-49 who think a husband has reason to beat or beat his wife under certain circumstances, for example, 87% in Mali, 86% in Guinea, 80% in the Central African Republic, 79% in South Sudan. Although many African countries now enact laws against domestic violence, social norms make it increasingly difficult to enforce them; and many women are unaware of their rights: for example in Ethiopia study only 49% of women knew that beating women was illegal (it was legalized under the 2004 Criminal Code). Lack of legal and social recognition of marital rape in Africa has been cited as making the fight against IV difficult.